Holi Festival of Color

by Grace Hansen

Abdo
WORLD FESTIVALS
Kids

Abdo Kids Jumbo is an Imprint of Abdo Kids
abdobooks.com

abdobooks.com

Published by Abdo Kids, a division of ABDO, P.O. Box 398166, Minneapolis, Minnesota 55439.
Copyright © 2023 by Abdo Consulting Group, Inc. International copyrights reserved in all countries.
No part of this book may be reproduced in any form without written permission from the publisher.
Abdo Kids Jumbo™ is a trademark and logo of Abdo Kids.

Printed in the United States of America, North Mankato, Minnesota.

102022

012023

Photo Credits: Alamy, Getty Images, Shutterstock
Production Contributors: Teddy Borth, Jennie Forsberg, Grace Hansen
Design Contributors: Candice Keimig, Pakou Moua

Library of Congress Control Number: 2021950562
Publisher's Cataloging-in-Publication Data

Names: Hansen, Grace, author.

Title: Holi festival of color / by Grace Hansen.

Description: Minneapolis, Minnesota : Abdo Kids, 2023 | Series: World festivals | Includes online resources
    and index.

Identifiers: ISBN 9781098261771 (lib. bdg.) | ISBN 9781098262617 (ebook) | ISBN 9781098263034
    (Read-to-Me ebook)

Subjects: LCSH: Holī (Hindu festival)--Juvenile literature. | Fasts and feasts--Hinduism--Juvenile literature.
    | Hinduism--Customs and practices--Juvenile literature. | Festivals--Juvenile literature. | Manners and
    customs--Juvenile literature.

Classification: DDC 394.2683--dc23

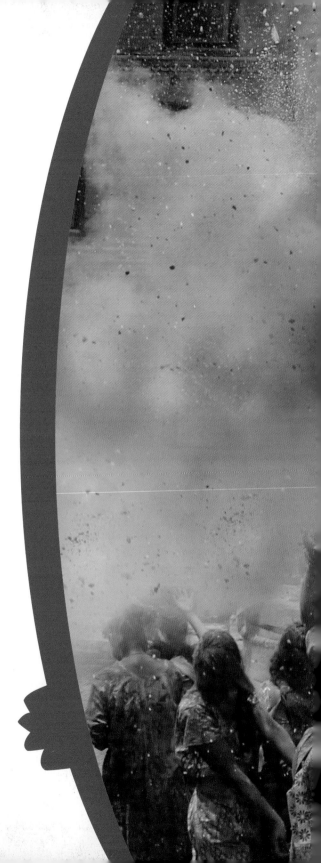

Table of Contents

Festival of Holi

Springtime is a colorful season throughout India and other parts of the world. This is when **Hindus** celebrate the famous festival of Holi.

Europe

Asia

Africa

India

Holi recognizes the end of winter and the start of spring and new life. Some **Hindus** hold religious **ceremonies** during Holi. There is also entertainment and food for all to enjoy.

Holi is celebrated on the full-moon day of the **Hindu** month of **Phalguna**. This day often lands sometime in March.

Holi History

Traditions surrounding Holi are rooted in Indian mythology. In many places, Holi is related to a legend of the evil King Hiranyakashipu. The king's son Prahlada worshipped the god Vishnu, which angered him.

Vishnu

11

The king asked his sister Holika to destroy Prahlada. Holika tricked Prahlada to sit with her on a pyre. She was supposed to be protected from the fire. Instead, Prahlada escaped while Holika burned.

Holika

Prahlada

13

Vishnu later defeated the king. It was a victory of good over evil. This is why the night before Holi, **pyres** are set on fire across India.

An incarnation of Vishnu
destroying the king

The Festival of Color

Many people relate Holi to the throwing of colored powder and water. This **tradition** comes from the story of Krishna and Radha. Krishna is a major **Hindu** god with blue skin. He is an **incarnation** of Vishnu.

The story goes that Krishna playfully smeared bright colors on Radha's face. The two then fell in love.

19

To celebrate this, people gather on Holi to sing and dance. They throw colored powder and water at one another. It is a fun and joyous occasion for all!

Some Holi Festival Foods

Puran Poli

Sweet, fried flatbreads stuffed with legumes and cane sugar or jaggery.

Pakora

Crispy fritters made with gram flour, spices and herbs, and vegetables such as onions and potatoes.

Gujiya

Dried dough pockets filled with khoya, jaggery, nuts, and raisins, and soaked in sugar syrup.

Thandai

A cold, milky drink made of nuts and spices such as fennel and cardamom.

Glossary

ceremony – a formal act or series of acts done in a particular way to honor a special occasion.

Hindu – a follower of Hinduism. Hinduism is the main religion of India, which has many gods that are part of the same supreme being.

incarnation – a person who embodies the flesh of a god or spirit.

Phalguna – a month of the Hindu calendar. It is the twelfth month of the year. It corresponds with February or March in the Gregorian calendar.

pyre – a stack of material, such as wood, used for burning something.

tradition – a long-established or inherited practice, such as an event.

Index

Abdo Kids
ONLINE
FREE! ONLINE MULTIMEDIA RESOURCES

Visit **abdokids.com**
to access crafts, games,
videos, and more!

Use Abdo Kids code
WHK1771
or scan this QR code!